This book belongs to

....

This book is dedicated to "The Four Amigos"
(C. Fredrick Milkie, MD, Shadi S. Sanbar, John Samore, Jr., and John M. Gantus)
for their ongoing encouragement and support.
Special thanks to: Doug Knox, Cliff Shiepe, Dennis Awad, John Maddex, and Khr Kimberly Taweel.
Spanish Translation: Khr Marcia O'Dea, Sonia Straghalis, Isabel Elac, and Fr Fadi Rabbat

Published by Candle Books
www.lionhudson.com
Part of the SPCK Group
SPCK, 36 Causton Street, London, SW1P 4ST
ISBN 9781781284346

First published in the USA in 2021 titled *The Wisdom of Padre Juan on True Riches*

A catalogue record for this book is available from the British Library
Produced on paper from sustainable sources

Printed and bound in China, November 2022, LH54

CANDLE
BOOKS

Written by
George Taweel

True
Treasures

Illustrated by
Anne Wertheim

Under a tree, on a hilltop,
are four children and a kindly man.

His eyes glitter and dance with joy.
His face is wrinkled with lines of laughter.
His heart is filled with love, as full as full can be.
His name is Brother John.

"Brother John, Brother John,
where is your house?"

"My roof is the stars...

My floor is the earth...

My windows overlook the mountains and the sea...

This is my house."

"Brother John, Brother John,
where are your treasures?"

"The flowers of the earth...

The birds of the sky...

The animals of the forest...

These are my treasures."

"Brother John, Brother John,
where is your Father?"

"I see Him in the radiance of the rainbow...

I hear Him in the song
of the whales...

I feel Him in the rays of His sun...

My Father is here, there, and everywhere."

"Brother John, Brother John,
why are you happy?"

"I am happy because I own nothing,
yet I possess everything.
I am empty, and yet I am full.
I have love, I have God, I have you!
This is why I am happy...

All the riches of this earth
are no more precious to me than YOU!"

"Brother John, Brother John,
WE LOVE YOU, TOO!"